The Life Cycle of Trees

by Gary Rushworth

Table of Contents

Pictures To Think About i
Words To Think About iii
Introduction 2
Chapter 1 The Beginning of a Tree 4
Chapter 2 The Growing Tree 10
Chapter 3 Life Cycles 14
Conclusion 22
Glossary 23
Index 24

Pictures To Think About

The Life Cycle of Trees

Words To Think About

Characteristics
- type of tree
- has leaves
- ?

deciduous
What do you think the word **deciduous** means?

Examples
- oak
- maple
- ?

photosynthesis
What do you think the word **photosynthesis** means?

Latin: *photo* (light)

Latin: *synthesis* (to mix together)

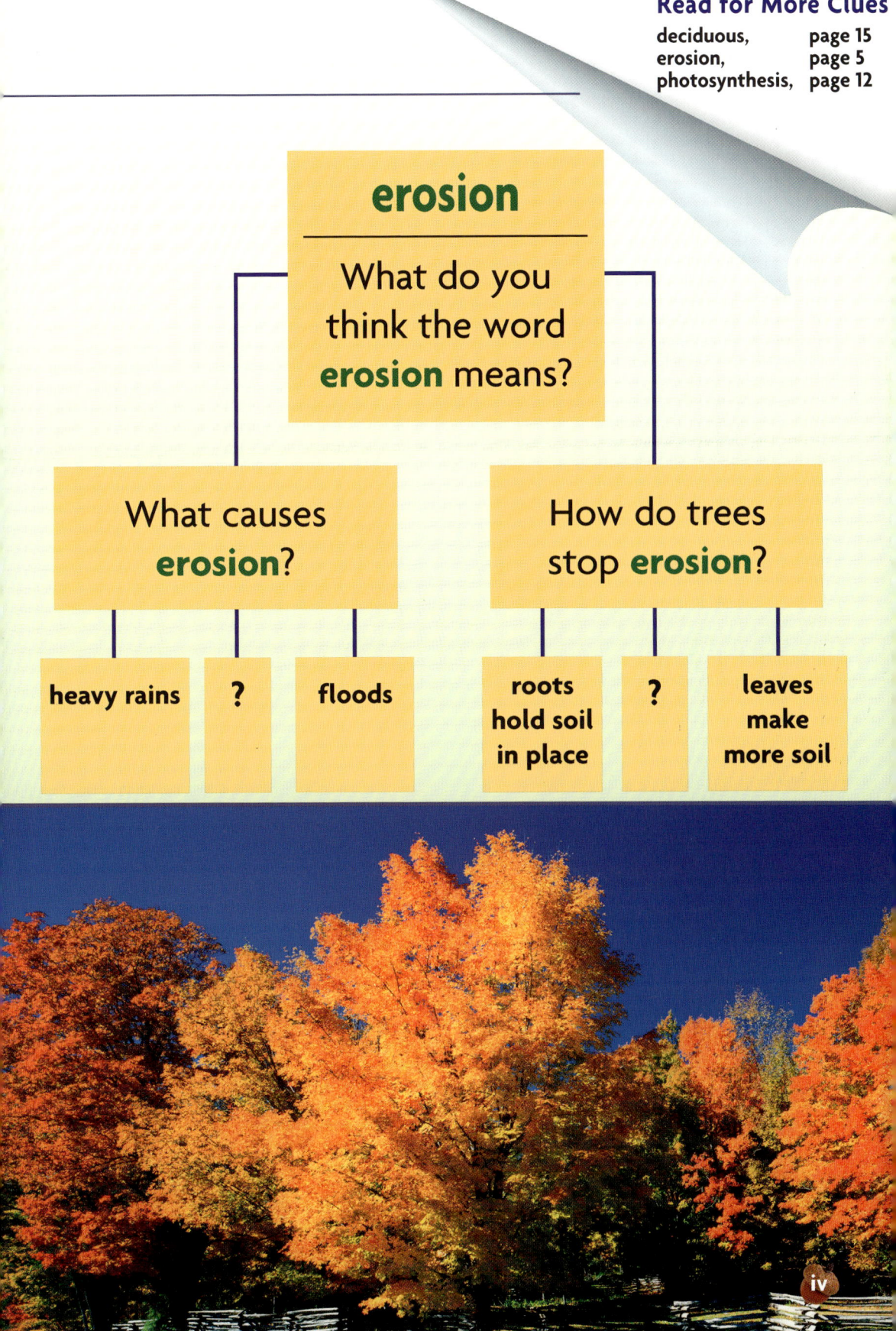

Introduction

Trees! Trees! Trees! We can see so many types of trees. Some trees are tall. Some trees are small. Some trees are green all year. Some lose their leaves in fall.

◀ It takes many trees to make a forest. This forest is in New Hampshire.

▲ Trees come in all sizes and shapes.

Trees Bring Life to Our World

Trees are important. Trees make the world a better place. Trees clean the air. Trees give food and shelter to living things. Trees make food that we eat, too. Can you think of fruits that grow on trees? Apples and peaches grow on trees. Many nuts grow on trees, too.

In this book, you will learn about how trees grow. You will learn why we need trees. You will also learn why trees need us! Read on. Learn about the life cycle of trees.

▲ We can hang a hammock between two trees.

▲ Trees provide habitats for many animals.

CHAPTER 1

The Beginning of a Tree

What is a tree? A tree is a plant. A young tree looks just like other small plants. A tree grows like other plants, too. However, a tree can grow much bigger than other plants. A tree can grow taller than a house.

The Life Cycle of a Tree Begins

Every tree starts as a **seed** (SEED). Even the biggest trees start as small seeds. Some trees can be more than 300 feet (91.44 meters) tall. These trees can grow more than 30 feet (9.14 meters) wide.

◀ The giant sequoia is one of the tallest trees. A sequoia starts out as a tiny seed.

Different Kinds of Seeds

Tree seeds come in all shapes, sizes, and colors. The seeds may look different, but they have the same job. Seeds grow into new trees.

A tree makes many seeds. Only a few of the seeds grow into trees. Many seeds die before they can grow. **Erosion** (ih-ROH-zhun) can kill seeds. Erosion happens when water washes away soil. Weather and fire can also kill seeds. Animals and humans can kill seeds, too.

▲ Seeds carry the information needed to make a new tree. The seed of every tree is unique.

▼ A tree makes many seeds, but only a few become trees. This is a young oak tree.

It's a Fact

The seed of a mustard tree is very small. Even so, mustard trees can grow to be more than 10 feet (3.04 meters) tall.

CHAPTER 1

All seeds have three main parts. All seeds have an **embryo** (EM-bree-oh). The embryo is the baby plant. All seeds have a **cotyledon** (kah-tih-LEE-dun). All seeds have a **seed coat** (SEED KOTE).

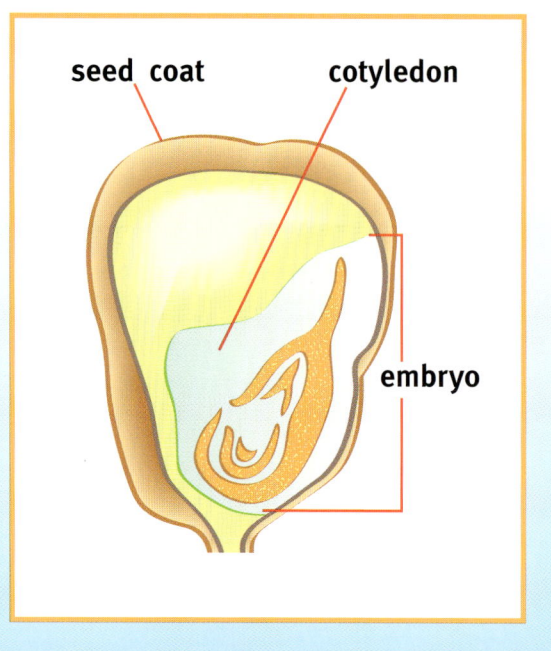

◀ Every seed has three parts.

THE BEGINNING OF A TREE

The cotyledon has food. This food helps the embryo grow.

The seed coat covers the seed. The seed coat protects the embryo.

Every seed needs water to grow. Every seed needs good soil to grow.

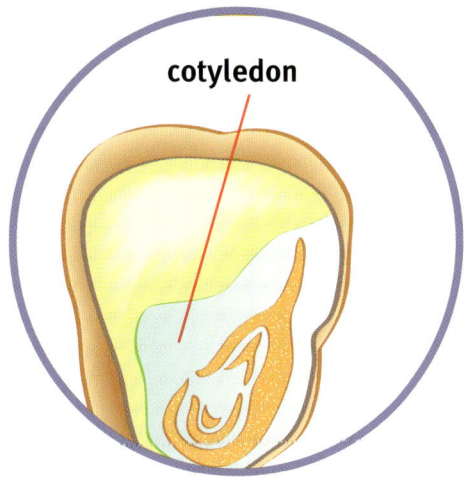

▲ The embryo, or baby tree, receives food from the cotyledon.

CHAPTER 1

▲ A tree trunk has several layers.

▲ It takes high winds like those of a hurricane to bend a tree.

Most plants have stems. A tree's stem is called the trunk. The trunk has layers. The tough outer layer is called bark. The bark covers and protects the trunk.

At first, the trunk is thin. As a tree grows, the trunk gets stronger and stronger. A grown tree does not bend with ease.

Historical Perspective

Early Native Americans made boats and canoes out of trees. Today some boats are still made of wood.

✓ POINT

Reread
Review the information about what a seed needs to grow and the dangers it encounters. Then make an inference about a tree you have noticed near your home or school.

THE BEGINNING OF A TREE

▲ These seedlings are on their way to becoming fully grown trees.

When a tree starts to grow, the stem pushes up out of the ground. The cotyledon is attached to the stem. The cotyledon feeds the baby tree.

Soon the leaves grow. Then the tree can make its own food. The cotyledon falls off.

CHAPTER 2

The Growing Tree

A tree needs good soil to make food. A tree also needs water, air, and light. These things keep a growing tree healthy.

Soil

Soil covers most of the land. Soil has tiny bits of sand and rock. Dead plants and animals are also in soil.

Soil can keep a tree from falling over. A tree gets nutrients (NOO-tree-ents) from soil. A tree gets water from soil, too.

EVERYDAY SCIENCE

Tree roots spread through the soil in search of water. When water is hard to find, the roots adapt. They make a chemical to prevent loss of water. Water is drawn into the roots but cannot leak out or evaporate.

▲ Floods and fast-moving water can wash the soil away.

Water

After it rains, water builds up in the soil. The tree's roots take water from the soil. Roots grow underground. Roots also keep trees in place.

Too much rain can cause erosion. Erosion is when soil washes away. Wind and waves cause erosion, too. Trees help stop erosion. The roots of trees hold soil in place.

CHAPTER 2

Light

A tree needs light to grow. A tree uses light to make food. This is called **photosynthesis** (foh-toh-SIN-theh-sis).

Photosynthesis

Photosynthesis happens inside leaves. Leaves need three things for photosynthesis. Leaves need **carbon dioxide** (KAR-bun di-AHK-side). Carbon dioxide is a gas in air. Leaves also need water. The roots send water up the trunk to the leaves. Leaves also need light. The light comes from the sun.

Inside the leaves, these three things mix. Then the leaves makes sugar. The tree uses the sugar for food. The leaves also let out a gas. The gas is **oxygen** (AHK-sih-jen).

▶ A tree absorbs carbon dioxide and releases oxygen through its leaves.

THE GROWING TREE

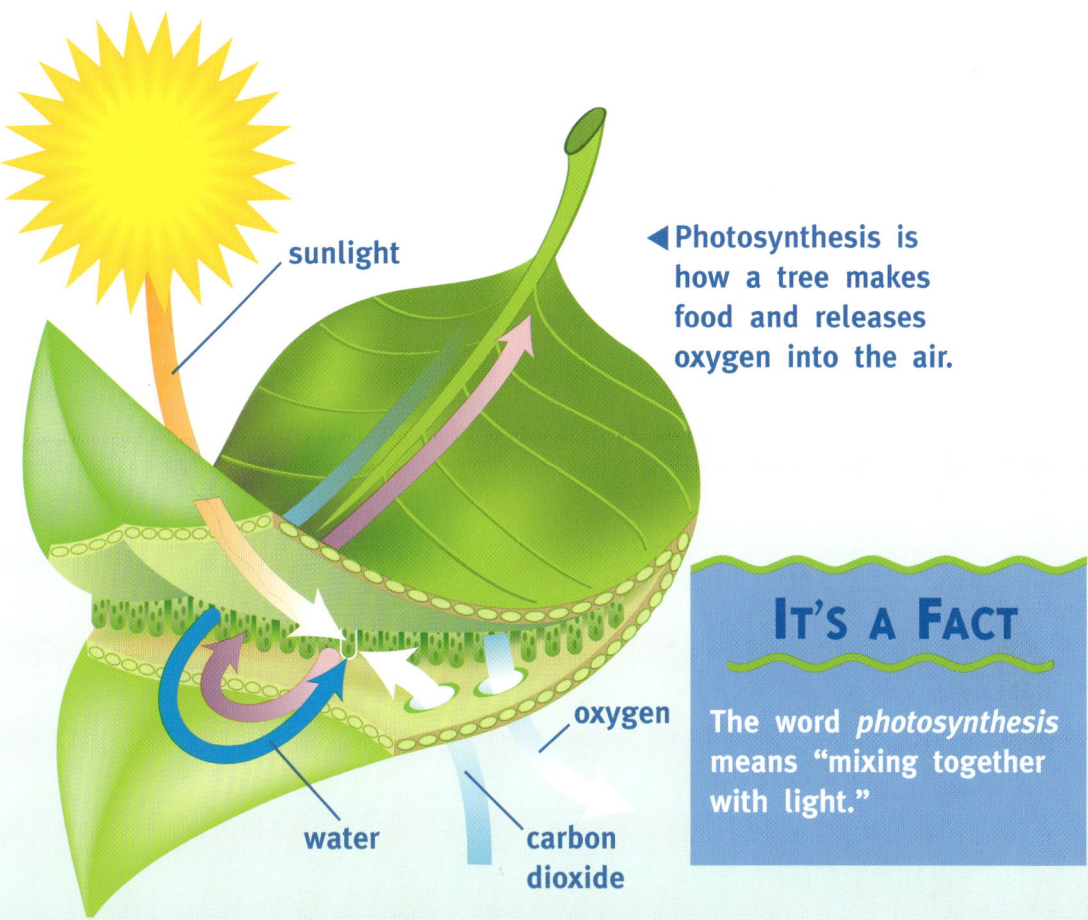

◀ Photosynthesis is how a tree makes food and releases oxygen into the air.

It's a Fact

The word *photosynthesis* means "mixing together with light."

All living things are connected. Trees and other plants make oxygen. Humans and other animals need oxygen to live. We breathe in oxygen from the air. Our bodies use oxygen to make energy. When we breathe out, we let out carbon dioxide. Trees and other plants use carbon dioxide. This cycle connects us all.

CHAPTER 3

Life Cycles

Earth has many types of trees. A **conifer** (KAH-nih-fer) is a tree with leaves shaped like needles. A pine tree is a conifer. Conifers hold their seeds in cones.

▲ Cones protect the seeds from damage.

▲ Evergreen trees are cone-bearing trees.

▼ Maple trees are deciduous.

A **deciduous** (dih-SIH-juh-wus) tree has broad leaves. Each year, new leaves grow, die, and fall off.

Most deciduous trees do not have cones. The seeds are under the leaves. When the seeds are ready, they drop off the tree. Some seeds land on soil. Those seeds may begin to grow.

▲ Maple tree seeds are like tiny helicopters. When they mature and fall from the tree, they spin until they land on the ground.

CHAPTER 3

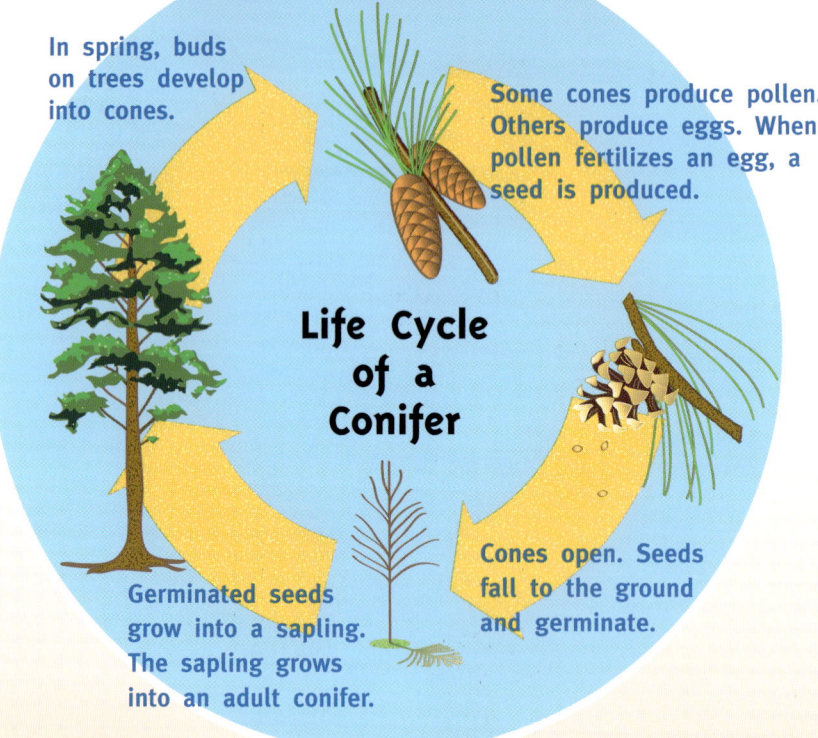

Life Cycle of a Conifer

A conifer is a tree that has cones. The tree's seeds are in the cones. When the cones open, the seeds fall to the ground. Some seeds may begin to grow where they fall. Other seeds are eaten by animals. The animals may travel far away. The seeds fall out in the animals' droppings. Those seeds can grow into new trees, too.

Conifers are known as evergreens. Evergreens stay green all year long. They are always losing and growing new leaves.

LIFE CYCLES

Life Cycle of a Deciduous Tree

Deciduous trees lose their leaves once each year. Oak is a deciduous tree. So are maple and elm. These trees lose their leaves in the fall. In the spring, the leaves grow back.

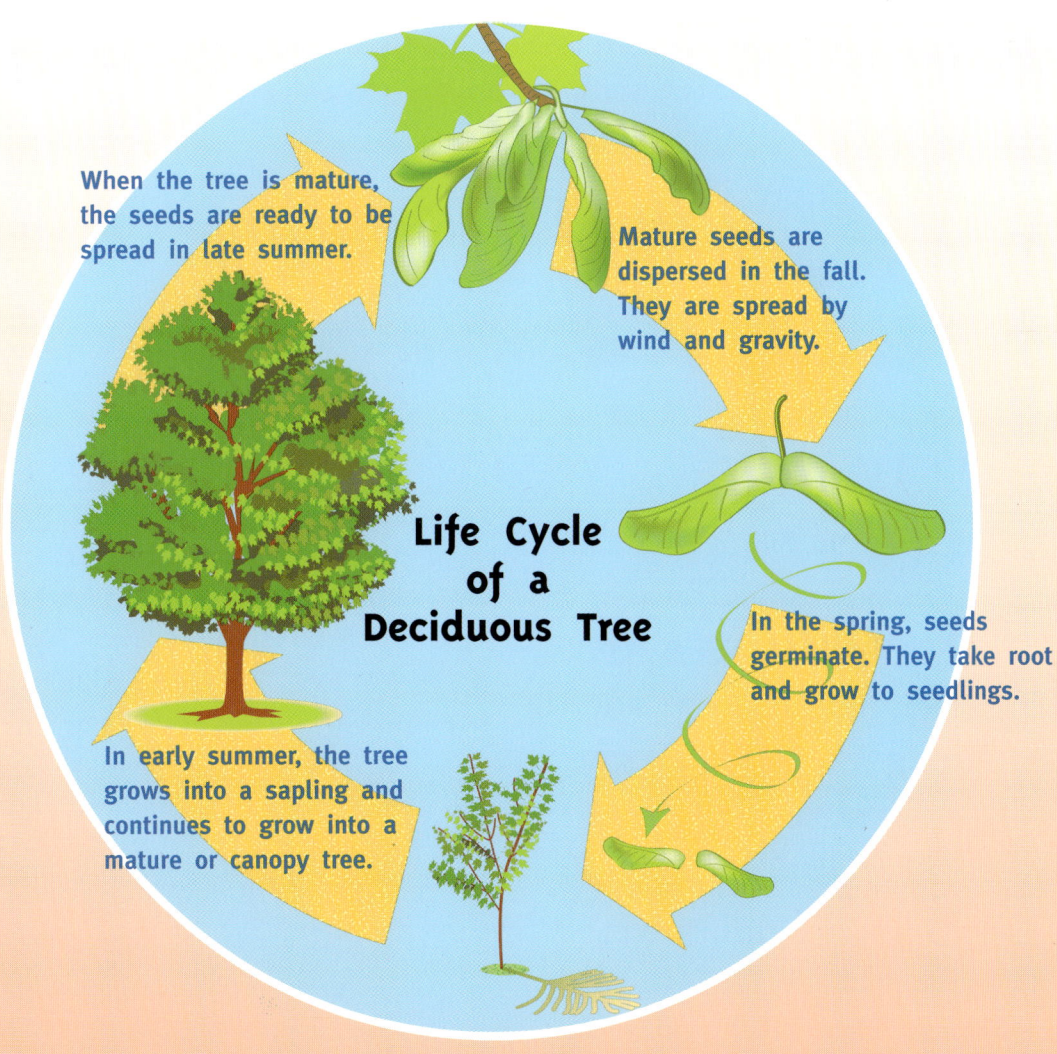

CHAPTER 3

▲ Fall can be a colorful season.

▲ Trees are fun to play on.

The Wonder of a Tree

A tree is a wonderful thing. A tree can give us food and shade. A tree can be a home for birds and other animals. A tree is also fun to climb!

EVERYDAY SCIENCE

We know the leaves of trees change colors in the fall. We see orange and red leaves. We see leaves that are brown and gold. But the green leaves are mostly gone. The truth is the colors were always there. We just couldn't see them.

Chlorophyll is a chemical that makes photosynthesis happen. Chlorophyll is also the chemical that makes leaves look green. As winter approaches, the amount of chlorophyll in the leaves is low, allowing the other colors of the leaves to show through.

LIFE CYCLES

Trees can live for a long time. Some trees live for thousands of years.

Tree rings (TREE RINGZ) tell the age of a tree. Each ring is equal to one year. Tree rings also tell us about the weather over time. If little rain falls in a year, the ring is very thin. If a lot of rain falls, the ring is wider.

▼ Tree rings tell how old a tree is. One ring equals one year, or cycle.

Everyday Science

Tree rings indicate the age of a tree. Each year, a new ring is added as the tree grows wider. The rings begin at the center of the tree and end where the bark begins.

CHAPTER 3

Trees have been around for billions of years. Trees are strong. But trees can be hurt and killed.

Forest fires kill many trees. Hot, dry weather causes some forest fires. Lightning causes other forest fires. People cause forest fires, too.

The oldest known living tree is a pine tree named Methuselah (muh-THOO-zuh-luh). It lives in the White Mountains of California. The tree is known to be forty-six centuries, or over 4,600 years old. This means the tree is older than the Egyptian pyramids.

▲ Methuselah

✔ POINT

Picture It

Pretend you're a grown-up tree. Draw a series of sketches that tell your life story. Add speech balloons to show what you would say in each sketch. In the last sketch, show what might happen to you in the future.

LIFE CYCLES

Good Forest Fires

A forest has brush, dead trees, and branches. These **forest fuels** (FOR-est FYOOLZ) can build up. Forest fuels burn quickly when they catch fire. They can cause big forest fires.

Forest rangers and firefighters try to get rid of forest fuels. To do this, they start a **comb fire** (KOME FIRE). A comb fire is a controlled fire. Comb fires burn away the forest fuels. Then workers put out the fire. Comb fires help stop forest fires.

▲ Comb fires help reduce the amount of forest fuels and help prevent big fires from spreading.

Conclusion

The life cycle of a tree begins with one seed. First, the roots form. Then the stem begins to grow.

As the stem, or trunk, grows, it gets a hard outer layer. This is called bark. Later, branches grow from the trunk. The branches grow leaves. Finally, the tree spreads seeds. Then the cycle begins again.

Trees are important. Trees make oxygen. Trees give food and shelter to animals. Humans eat many foods that grow on trees. We use wood from trees to build our homes. We even use trees to make paper and pencils.

Together, we can keep Earth green with trees. Start by planting a tree every year!

Glossary

carbon dioxide (KAR-bun di-AHK-side) a gas used by trees in photosynthesis (page 12)

comb fire (KOME FIRE) a controlled fire used to burn away forest fuels between trees (page 21)

conifer (KAH-nih-fer) a cone-bearing tree (page 14)

cotyledon (kah-tih-LEE-dun) the first food source for trees and plants (page 6)

deciduous (dih-SIH-juh-wus) leaf-producing trees that lose all their leaves during part of the year (page 15)

embryo (EM-bree-oh) baby plant within a seed (page 6)

erosion (ih-ROH-zhun) washing away of soil and rocks by rain and floods (page 5)

forest fuel (FOR-est FYOOL) brush that builds up between trees in the forest (page 21)

oxygen (AHK-sih-jen) a gas that we breathe, which is released by trees during photosynthesis (page 12)

photosynthesis (foh-toh-SIN-theh-sis) the process trees use to make food from water, carbon dioxide, and light (page 12)

seed (SEED) the part of a plant that contains the embryo, cotyledon, and seed coat (page 4)

seed coat (SEED KOTE) the outer protective covering of a seed (page 6)

tree ring (TREE RING) ring that reveals the age of a tree (page 19)

Index

carbon dioxide, 12–13

comb fire, 21

conifer, 14, 16

cotyledon, 6–7, 9

deciduous, 15, 17

embryo, 6–7

erosion, 5, 11

evergreen, 16

forest fuel, 21

leaves, 2, 9, 12–13, 15, 17, 18, 22

oxygen, 12–13

photosynthesis, 12–13

seed, 4–7, 14–17, 22

seed coat, 6–7

tree ring, 19